D1050238

SCAFFOLDING

PRINCETON SERIES OF CONTEMPORARY POETS

Susan Stewart, *series editor*

For other titles in the Princeton Series of Contemporary Poets see page 85

SCAFFOLDING

Poems

Eléna Rivera

PRINCETON UNIVERSITY PRESS
Princeton and Oxford

Copyright © 2017 by Princeton University Press

Published by Princeton University Press, 41 William Street,
Princeton, New Jersey 08540

In the United Kingdom: Princeton University Press, 6 Oxford Street,
Woodstock, Oxfordshire OX20 1TR

press.princeton.edu

Jacket image courtesy of Russell Switzer

Library of Congress Cataloging-in-Publication Data
Names: Rivera, Eléna, author.
Title: Scaffolding : poems / Eléna Rivera.
Description: Princeton : Princeton University Press, [2017] | Series: Princeton series
of contemporary poets
Identifiers: LCCN 2015049660| ISBN 9780691172262 (softcover : acid-free paper)
| ISBN 9780691172255 (hardcover : acid-free paper)
Classification: LCC PS3568.I8292 A6 2017 | DDC 811/.54--dc23 LC record
available at http://lccn.loc.gov/2015049660

British Library Cataloging-in-Publication Data is available

This book has been composed in Adobe Garamond Pro and ScalaSansOT

Printed on acid-free paper. ∞

Printed in the United States of America

10 9 8 7 6 5 4 3 2 1

SEPT. 3ʳᵈ AFTER JACQUES ROUBAUD

she likes to write her sonnets on La Salle Street
where the saw keeps her company and her words
on this great city stage are nothing concrete
just a door that swings open wings flap the birds

eat her sandwich in Central Park very near
the Delacorte where the play is *Midsummer*
though it's no longer June light now disappears
on the crowd who eat and drink by the river

all disappear afterward south to Times Square
where "living" means the glare/"dare" of the night shift
like the poets and their stupendous affair

with St. Marks, the Bowery and catching a rift
here there herself the sound of the city's flare
as the lines shift and she sets the lines adrift

Contents

SCAFFOLDING

JULY 14TH FROM 80 LA SALLE

Dawn in the city, windows wide open—wham!
Slam! Screams! Now scaffolding confronts this hometown—
trash smashed, strollers, birds, doors opening/closing
Here happens, all day, tending to tones sounding
in our ears—Beep! Vehicle backs into street
veers round the corner—listen, take note of this
city waking, summer moistened with sirens,
syncopated noise—beats anticipate stress
as skyscrapers vibrate—"All's well," you say, "All's
Here"—a car idles, shakes, feeds the vertigo—
water the balcony's garden, hear children,
hear the blaring radio counterpoint to
the modest breeze this morning—back inside then,
at the desk, the sawed railings of the poem

JULY 30TH

The dictionary the eye the ear our lungs
open, engender "owl" here "genesis" there
Turn the page and all things come alive echo
in the imagination—the word leads us
into worlds into time into reverie—
And the real? what happens to reality?
No need for Derrida, the deconstruction
already part of the city's laws where we
live leave everything to measure re-measure
Construction and destruction, bricks are replaced
Without answers without frame the scaffolding
highlights the slab the bricks the mortar playpen,
not just whispers but its cinder block questions
From drill to hammer to threshold to discourse

JULY 31ST SHELL-WORDS

I put you together, fall in with the past,
return to fading atmospheres no matter
the pillars, columns, moments evaporate
Mourn the loss of light poet you wrote of this
not a new notion we look back always look
the woman tripped, fell, her head hitting concrete,
shocked by the body that aging monument
One page faces another where poets look
at shadows, illuminate the present place
The multitude must be in the words, allude
to the boundless past that sentence that binds us
crashes into liberty's baffling riddle
Boulders, ocean, and the old obscurity
What happened to them, us, writing in water?

AUG. 5TH

When a man is asked to sing of his anger
the risk is that without remorse virtue dies
War then is in the face, in this homelessness,
the despair which couldn't wait couldn't ask for

We don't talk to each other anymore we
email global reach managed minutes morning
to noon in the hospitals we are all old
forbidden to talk of lost sons, asked to smile

Enough, they'll hear the news, men in photographs
die and nothing will seem simple, their faces
especially where sorrow stretched everything

Maps point to? and defeat looms where? out there where?
Here the naked body is where terror lies
Guilt builds monuments, the way we spend our time

AUG. 8ᵀᴴ FOR THOMAS HARDY (REVISED JUNE 5ᵀᴴ)

If we say it's all up to chance do we mean
a throw of dice or an unexpected risk?
Can we bear being battered with sorrow, joy?
Contingent one moment on calamitous
headlines, another by the fear of our death
Obliterated by confrontation—Job's
test? And if "Un coup de dés" then Mallarmé's
"le hasard" sits at a piano in a room—
Nothing but "crass casualty" obstacles these
obstructions that cover the rising of light
in the East—the painter's eye tailored by light
shares with us a gladness for color and sun
We need new angles from which to see look out
the window, there in the garden the gamble

AUG. 9TH

WAITRESS

The uniform the stockings the waiting, time
to carry the tray balanced for the banquet
Maroon and pink polyester with black shoes
"Cygne" or "swan" rushing across the ballroom floor
The pigeon place where the assembled come to
pick at steaks, filet mignon, ten per table,
swallowed between dances bold sweep of it or
left behind in the trash where no one can dine
Avenue block ballroom I crash into space
myself nothing a figure crossing the room
emptied of person and picking up glasses
The servers all speak different languages
Not there to sing with a lyre but to pour drinks
until the clock strikes midnight and we disperse

STARTED AUG. 11TH (FINISHED FEB. 20TH)

Being there one is struck by the difference
that an ocean makes—the park advertises
"How it used to be" charges admission sells
"Nostalgia" and "History" to the tourist

"Le passant's" aim is to complicate a view
To fulfill this pleasure a guide explicates
the art of falconry; its role in Britain

The family returns to the car, the hotel,
the next meal, finished with that site, surrounded
by a thin remembrance of a falcon's stare

A family "en route" revealed, translating
signage, instructions, "the way we used to be"
Struck by the absence of accompaniment
and what one can say in another country

AUG. 12TH WITH WORDSWORTH

What a surprise the fresh breeze, noticing it
Golden euphoria and wham! a strong wind
ever ready behind small experience
Words will latch on to air if you let them grab
burrow their way stick have you think you are it
Eenie meenie miney moe and the sweat drips
the shirt clings to memory clings years ago
And when you least expect it it all comes back
I'm at a window elated by the sky
the moment where lights branched out and I was small
A day where fireworks competed with lightning
We in the big city in our huge smallness
rushing in out of the bodega for beer
and chips cigarettes and "real" celebration

AUG. 13TH

The mind gets overfull on certain mornings
Maybe that's the way of the scribe to forage
and scour (note that trying to protect oneself
from language makes for a longing to comply
with wind-blown anger, impossible of course)
An aunt's stern eye turns into tugs in the mind
You can look up, instantly feel your wrongness,
how the fear of lost fondness undoes the mind
Hours elapsed, days, years, no breeze in the heat
Children then grew fearful of shadows and dark
Adults feel their passel memories heat cheeks,
"by the fall of a shadow across the ground"
The "pollution tolerant" Lindens and Oaks
witness our delusion, we work in the dark

AUG. 14TH

The form carries a one-way conversation,
site of separation brought into relief
A relationship between sonnet and "house"
the I that tried to run away, walls of snow,
and how invisible the girl felt, small, bold

Wordsworth would never scorn the form, his ground O
it would take me years to kowtow to this earth
quake and still resist the good loam, the concrete
world, think of man's enlightenment, follow paths
of beauty of sound of ideas and then dreams

The struggle for a way out, a faith in this,
through the house, past deaf-ears, into the snow filled
One forgets that the form is, a lamp transports
Oh the cold has clearly entered the sonnet

AUG. 15ᵀᴴ FOR WILLIAM SHAKESPEARE

To have the kind of _____ that no one can   presence
That will not hurt ____ even the smallest thing   not
I saw a fly, now _____ circle around leaves   gnats
That will not judge or cradle the cold or _____   turn

The self in this has no grace, ____ gratitude,   no
thinks boredom the barrier when it's ____ gold,   pure
energizes _____ jumps hoops just for grace,   matter
if sweet _____ our fellow gardenias and herbs   gives

We think of things as _____, correction   reflection
The sweet can fester instead __ the human   of
When divided it's ___ surface that rankles   the
with pain at the gate of self and its _____   structures

Poet remind me it's more _____ than need   subtle
She crosses her legs circled around the _____   leaves

AUG. 16TH

Seeped in a nineteenth century piety

I see how I forgot to strip them the sounds
molded by my father's Eliot records
I see your method sticks to spoken language
cannot face or gauge every word in my head
I would stumble against the choir the grand voice
the sloppiness that I would be punished for
At eleven we don't think of what words say
In the twenty first century I desire
form that pushes the limits of silty thought—
the long and flexible so I can surprise
your privacy (I almost wrote "piracy"),
describe your spine curving slightly as I bend
back the pages, his soft freckled hand on mine

A̶U̶G̶.̶ ̶1̶8̶ᵀᴴ (VERSION 2)

He came out of the sea to greet mere mortals
Poseidon of the Mediterranean
The man I admired had no permanence,
he would always go back to where he came from
so the children thought when the world was color
There's a picture of the God in his swimsuit
hair floating, in profile, ready to surface,
but the past and the wet red rage container
saw the sea lion move from place to place, un-
tethered and the children watched his sheen rub off
in a dark apartment his sea charm broken
tethered to "responsibilities" bursting
with rage, smashed a catsup bottle into bits
as the world's color changed into black & white

AUG. 19TH

This year tangled up in last year transported
The mistake that we make of time occurring,
future fast-forwarding never quite finding
Ladybugs all we can ask of the living,
and of sonnets, when they get claustrophobic
Always have to have a very high idea
of what we do, how we end up "being" time
Do we tell others what or do we write words
This year lived in expectations nothing I
could wear and the past has a way of catching
Summer sky can be very blue the day cold,
picked up mistakes one by one, can you blame me
There were no rules, no regulations, nothing,
no wonder I felt trapped by the lack of them

AUG. 20ᵀᴴ

Inasmuch as you let materials mask
a thought attaches and words adhere to you,
merry-go-round of constructions and of noise
Is knowledge of the phone ringing essential
specially when the view draws your eyes forward
Stein tried to show the mystery of pattern
short scenes with titles (big words we learn later)
I was attacked from all sides worrying about
what was said, in me those slabs with words on them
Masking tape exposure, scissors, stones, paper
Basically my error was in holding back
and judging when I was in the thick of it
like looking at a filmstrip splicing takes place
At a cellular level everything linked

AUG. 21ST

I penetrated the narrative, had to
engage the pigment of the perpetrator

No quick confession here just the taking on
of various elements, showing the world steps

Because I can't separate myself from them
"because we are here," now, my siblings, my self

How a "tale" is perceived by a child of nine,
how brute force is perceived by an audience,

how revenge is never an option because
pierce that world and pleasure escapes, totally

Clearly the idea of fairness was a sham
The failure of not being able to see

and most blindness turns to imitation not
being, the real fiction needs an audience

AUG. 22ND

Absent again from all that really matters
The pendulum swings back and forth from a branch
—memory of being proud of the father
swinging from a rope the child admiring him
Depend on the clock to keep you hanging there
On the bus a few were left behind tick tock
Sit cross-legged, try to breathe, that was the talk
that introduced the teenager to the way,
the deserted path up and down from the beach
The instruction was to just "do it" as if
a piece of meat sitting there at the table
Annoyed by everything, wore black, erupted,
she painted herself in shades of vermilion
From lava to slag the answer is tick tock

AUG. 23RD FOR COLERIDGE

Always at work even when we don't work our
"nature" "stirring" the pages that appear air
winter words, worries and the same appetite
for pushing the smile away wearing our spiel
a similar sort of indolence I know
but making assumes, hopes, clarity will come
And what if what we do is afflicted with
"the real world" reflecting back a lack, grim news,
a place that gains nothing from Job-like efforts?
Even without hope we must still bide our time,
wait as the bloom waits for sunshine this chance to
indulge in giving what we do, we must "work
without hope" and traipse in the woods, this too is
necessary, not indolent, for "nectar"

AUG. 26TH FOR INGER CHRISTENSEN

To allow them to keep coming, to want to
remember the lavender rosemary thyme
in the hills, in the salt, tasting the thick heat
Here the scent of the Mediterranean

Childhood's playground of dirt and heat, a spider
blocks the path, black and yellow stripes, eye level
In that moment a butterfly fluttering
Children listen, wait for the ride to the beach

Heat heavy, don't step on the ants, be careful
The car burns the family and all complain
Memories blend spent midday by the warm sea
They'll clamor out of the car and buy Fanta

All memories are seas and words thicken them,
cornstarch for the brain, country bread for body,
don't drown in the grip of loss, float, use your fan

AUG. 27ᵀᴴ

. . . gets lost in identification with loss—
the surface so tense that it breaks the body . . .
Cough, choke, faint, fall, then all the talk around it
You peeled the orange in a spiral and laughed

Brittle words, the same old story, the meanness,
you laughed at my expense and I took it in—
bring me a blue coat to blanket and clear doubt
In the fields bleeding hearts flower in the spring

The spiral, the scent, is now no longer here
but emotions make museums of our thoughts
We are caught in between, in the crevice, in
a cardboard box, "dead in a box," or Alive

The city crocuses were ready, eager
Your secret crap was buried between the cracks

AUG. 28TH

The deeper one goes, the greater the surface
gleaned now that destruction of architecture,
of fragments, of traces, of the sun, the day,
and the rays that reflect the color of things

Violence and its values shatter a place
Newsflash and its follow-up not a site to
linger in flabbergasted as they are by
the bilingual gasped in a cycle of loss

In the manicured foot a callous has grown
The hardened childlike rhythm part of the plan
where the references are already anchored

On the promenade or from a great height our
pale thoughts intent on deciphering our end
The clean smell of grass after a long downpour

AUG. 29TH

The saw the hammer and the worry again
Stayed up late to listen to the candidate
Kick the leg up and then hit it with both hands
She doubled her efforts without making it
What goes on outside the body essential
The subway's here, hurry to your destruction
The doctor told the woman not to worry
No cause yet I couldn't understand the rest
Sandals and the movement of the feet in them
The man on the high wire walked back and forth
Smiled when seeing revealed the unexpected
Had requested a thing without naming it
The t'ai chi teacher spoke in Chinese and kicked
She expected something more from her father

AUG. 31ST

What does it mean "the poem unfamiliar"?
What about the new they ask what is the new
Rimbaud frozen in the desert some ate him
It's a ping-pong game of familiar patterns

We need intimations of _____ (plug in the word)
To take advantage of other routes today
A birch tree in winter illuminated
By sunlight I mean taking advantage of

Childish things without meaning I'd vote for them
He who wants to listen grows polyphonic
In strange ways this is the time to hold the door

The drama of the aural is in our mouth
Day after day we insist on this speaking
Meaning "wider"—is that the self the ear hears?

SEPT. 1ST

What is certain when many thoughts *brouilles les pistes*
That breath is present amid *le mot, le verbe*
Don't tell me you don't see the correspondence
There's French and English and counting syllables
Choose your cover, obscured on either side then
The paradox that comes from too much reading
Don't try to stop my hand it rose and disposed
Of so many lines so many breaks and sounds
A tickle in my throat—Must water the plant—
It comes back the present no matter the time
Black and white does not capture the gradations
What is possible in bands of thin red lines
Tried to meditate, tried to negotiate
"I write to keep alive" Who said that? I did

SEPT. 5TH

time slips away and it's all been done before
they say, and if i could change big emotions
into a song like Wyatt's what small joy then
the fitting of these wild pieces together—

the fragments of silence out of which sounds rise
claim attention, though many persons turn from
this, wear headgear to cancel this density
build themselves these tall structures to hide behind

i want the sunlight to see what is in front,
the magnetic small word written for a world
that slips away in a dream and reappears

when i seek what i don't really remember—
i was caught in its embrace and now it's gone,
the watchword slips away and i keep searching

SEPT. 9TH THE TRANSLATION

"To read what is hidden" the conversation
begins with that, the silence, the cloaked waiting
It must be paid attention to no matter
what—it demands to be first as is its right,
and too much accretion woven around it
will hide instinct's way if ego's unwilling
to bond with, to taste the dialogue's intense
distance—that entering of mind's divisions,
bringing one tongue forward reading the other's
silence without unraveling completely,
having a sense of direction a desire
to meet the poem's density where thickness
clings to a cloaked rendering that doesn't end
but meets with isolated words: tuff, gorse, edge

SEPT. 10TH NONE DONNE SONNET

Not a "little world made cunningly" just cut
from scrap metal torn for a stanzaic flight
of fancy—restless embryo reaching light—
though words can't camouflage for the most part the
late-summer dust, the turn toward music stays tuned
to the genesis of presence, the dream gift
an image that turns the seventh line into
morning when mourning gives rise to fourteen lines—
Here zeal is stored in part behind thoughts resides
in memories brought out by certain word cues—
How the man left the woman waiting crying
How fits of lust burned, earned with listening to
legacies of hurt instead of to robins,
warblers, an angel, sparrows, finches, starlings

SEPT. 11TH MORNING SONNET

The yoga teacher died didn't know her well—
draped over a bolster my lungs filled with air
as she adjusted my back—that blissful touch
Sunshine on lake, ripples wrinkle the surface

Thoughts of breakfast palpable feelings of
anger/hunger distracted then by mental
drama the pastime shaped wandering—"Send my
roots rain" Hopkins wrote, solemn obsecration

On the porch I read a medieval romance,
sentences towering over the water
Silence in room of pastoral proportions

Man in a motorboat on the lake lurches,
unsettles the silence and rips the sheen off—
Note: the watch is on the plastic tablecloth

SEPT. 12TH FOR GEORGE HERBERT

A small stretch to test the range of residence—
does it matter how long one's been a tenant?
I thrive off your words and am far from rescued
to suit anyone so send up the butcher
that sold me that small new lease with no release
To become spellbound in children's rhymes, reach for
that moment when earth speaks for the murderer,
where the written _is_ land _is_ body _is_ thief—
redemptive being enchanted by patterns
according to no measure just light gladness—
In all the riffs the surface is clean, but deep
in the lake, the forests, seas, the good rescue
is actually best when the day is wrested
and something is understood of crookedness

SEPT. ~~15~~ᵗᴴ (REVISED JULY 19ᵀᴴ, FINISHED JAN. 22ᴺᴰ)

for Michael Palmer

Not to mention form, emotion, being in
New York now city of subjects and effects
stilled only by the instant of a painting
or hearing about war in the news that night
Add judgment and the harvest is full of lies

The people say they choose, so we desire
childhood just one space to draw from, a small room,
a portrait without color, route, reduced to
a book, an idea of self in passing

Couldn't quite separate myself from others
What I mean when I say "certain structures" stick
to the city's harbor swollen with motion
the word faces the sun which melts the stage not
the tension between window and barricade

SEPT. 17ᵀᴴ (FINISHED JULY 20ᵀᴴ)

Language and memory and forgetfulness
The word means something and is not forgiving
In the mirror she sees her mind form a twin
The thing thus signified has now a new name
Names in one language sometimes resemble names
in the other she notes powers of recall
Memory's portrait not the sonnet's portrait
Limited by fourteen lines and conclusions
The power of the poem to understand
An attempt to pinpoint that "point de repère"
I remember she said and the others said
No, don't force other events, occurrences
came out as if it were in some way fractured
I forgot absence and it rooted itself

SEPT. 18TH FOR PERCY BYSSHE SHELLEY

A traveler gathers parts and combines them,
carries the fragments forward (if possible)—
On every lip a whisper to that effect—
Its lyrical sculpture made lakes of your world
in white marble memory and in pale words
A record of absence (kept scrupulously),
being that the mind can move carelessly and
keep fretting, the motion of upright pillars,
the state of barely breathing, just barreling
through, and hubris which swallows all the others
They fall by the wayside though—we live combined,
hyphens between two dates and mutual fear
So mustn't lose track of the balance and fall
apart break up each time traveling takes you

SEPT. 19TH POEM FOR ALICE 1

She turns her head, recites   ". . . the houses are all
going"—they're shadows now, neighborhood expunged
        ". . . see a house brought down/like a hunted creature"
A double-backed house, before the highways came,

and waxen white magnolias on a porch where
friends called to hear stories about ancestors,
the tales of a place   "where murdered beauties hang"
on a porch on Calliope Street, New Orleans—

The voice of a city that in fact needed
tales of   "facade gardens,"   "electric flowers,"
of times gone by, Alice recalled hot summers—

Cars collide, horns blast, jackhammers drill their holes
She watched a streetcar slowly go round a bend
Talks, writes about New Orleans   "gone/the houses . . ."

SEPT. 20TH POEM FOR ALICE 2 (REVISED N.D.)

Today go out to the cafeteria
Long silvery hair in a big bun on top
Tortoiseshell comb—Calvin "is going to work"
watch, chain, suspenders—80 degrees at 8
The familiar theme about Sonny why he . . .
Each blaming the other: A says C too hard
Tomorrow going trout and croaker fishing
Then all order dessert, 4 the hottest time
Talks about the old place on Calliope Street,
about what a great fisherman Sonny was
Tips the waiter modestly, remembers him
Several did not get to Louisiana
Many complaints about not driving safely
News comes in, then there's the usual argument

SEPT. 22ND

Certain stories travel, others dragon dreams
No trace of telling just faint hints of Spenser
Seeing father's penis, the wiry black hairs
Years later that's what assonance would look like
Told to "loosen up" but frightened of insects
Backward and forward not knowing what to feel
Riches hidden, sought around every corner
Every prince a man forcing himself, his "rod"
In out the words piled on top of the story
Wanted it, the body yearned for something fine
Shoes thrown in a corner, a single mattress
A rock idolized in high school on top hairs
Taking her while her mind latched on to a script
A film of the knight and forever after

SEPT. 24ᵀᴴ

Top of the tree, a place to settle the eye—
troubled by the way the dolls stayed suspended
Didn't disappear which was what the two girls
wanted, the grand-aunt's gift to disappear—she
who read Defoe and also gave chocolates
The dolls were discarded not "dropped" as lies were,
and her angry hurt words, "Why did you throw them?"
That night the large figure making the sign of
the cross on our foreheads where guilt was written—
the shame and pleasure of willfulness—Crusoe,
these dolls, and chocolate, all out of order
even if other "small" "thin" dolls flourished in
the small girls' thoughts, they darted to the bottom
ashamed as the dolls hung on eloquently

SEPT. 25TH

WHAT IS IT ABOUT IRREVERENCE YOU ASK?

"Mind your own business" said mind to its tailor
"Tough going this sonnet business" said ego
to its neighbor "We're not talking of a fight,
we're talking about sincerity, putting
one's all in the song" "Is that all? Figures, thought
you meant to give up your center to enter"
"You might want to rephrase that in the future"
"Never" "Nobody said change would be easy"
"In known periods of transition beware of
grief known at times of departures to ensnare
one unawares" "We were trying to assuage
here" "You said 'all'" "I said 'putting one's all in'"
"Figures, I thought boredom would curb you" "I'm back
at the entrance, let the virtual line begin"

SEPT. 29TH

Old stone house, no running water, spiders, mice
Everything dry, heat rises, winds blow dust, burns
the metal of the car, the nearby beach—oh
have to get in the car if they want to go
to the beach, and parents not speaking again—
"Après on ira acheter du pain au
village"—nothing but anticipation for now,
the water, sand, Fanta, multicolored flags,
the ice cream (can barely contain ourselves), run!
They're at the beach in August, mother reading,
father runs after them laughing then diving,
a Greek god for a while until new rage grabs
—in the end and on her own she watches as
her brother and sister build their sandcastles

SEPT. 30TH

in front of altars sat all enthralled before
art is the reason the smell of marigolds
a cardboard comfort this making this needing
the energy there in your body could heal

cares come when caring at stake so caring *is*,
worries *are* a metronome wipe the windshields
practically speaking people need their parts
again a question of not waiting for things

all asking is a form of farming, first ask
then plant poetries, presence a possible
conversation and start new ways of thinking

look i'm little enough to be erased so . . .
a sparrow picked twigs, i picked locks in language
"until peace comes" in gold or showy yellow

OCT. 1ST

"I love," the rest of the sentence acts on it
"love a dog's delight, the way it wags its tail"
Look up is the image enough for the mind
or is there need for "the story of my life"?
The words need to come together carefully,
lines an instrument of thought not otherwise
Learned English the hard way, crashing into "what"
"should" "this" contiguous or void, holding hands
and being speechless, my being so, wanting
luck and love, not to be deceived by language
All beauty is an instance of attention
Turn to the shuffling woman in the subway,
"Help me please" she says "have a heart" all that is
required is restored in minutes, act on it

OCT. 2ND

Cross the Lethe by subway with its bootless
cries I learned to twist my tongue at the office
Heart in a can, at a desk, large glass windows
Let the world in light doesn't just console it
reminds us of the babble that went before—
the growth of calluses that came from landing
at lunchtime between buildings sandwich in hand
Henceforth pulling weeds, one moment on a bus
the other slow to move, slow to confess, slow
to progress, stuck at the breast holds a paycheck,
wound in a story, wound of the sugared clock,
timed by one foot in print, the other in place
City good for making cookie-cutter types
Timed the return of evening ate everything

OCT. 3RD (VERSION 1)

surface ellipses . . . a kind of tropism . . .
it always depends on the definition—
Fragaria "wild strawberry" noun and root
and perhaps, more and more, torn by lack of time
for ecstasy—we are tempted (you see this
everywhere, hear of its little importance)
point to poetry, the place where the parts *are!*
(instead of living the parenthetical)
(instead of this race toward emptiness, this race
that masks our insignificance, our "false fruit")
(judgment too repeatedly wears us out our
seeds, I heard "What do you expect at your age")
(the early stages of metamorphosis)
she bit into the soft sweet red fruit and missed

~~OCT. 3~~ᴿᴰ (VERSION 2, REVISED N.D.)

Surface tension, growth . . . a kind of tropism . . .
the early stages of metamorphosis
depend on the body and definition—
Fragaria "wild strawberry" noun and root—
Remind the young girl tempted by ecstasy
that fantasy is a fragrance, shame clings to
the changes of the body—blood running down
and pee pushed her to the parenthetical—
That weighing in, comparing size shape, the change
How games put forward the questions of "better"
and fruit when bruised by too much judgment retreats
"What do you expect at your age"—early stage—
then came to poetry, the place where parts *are*
is a soft sweet red fruit that I missed and miss

OCT. 7TH "CONFESS THAT IT IS SO"

To see oneself around age seven enraged—
feet stamp the ground the story of violence
sealed, virtue a mask made at a later date
(plucked eyebrows, painted cheeks, mascara, lip gloss)
This period is called "dry" so even sheep find
no possible growth, ancestor anger *is*—
that all resistance just builds more resistance
and like Antigone one takes up the noose
for the sibling whose way was one of hunger
Light cannot penetrate the cave of a child
when the ending of it all seems possible
To keep seeing oneself age seven enraged—
nobody no one found out nobody knew,
coat and scarf checked, everything else was staging

~~OCT. 8~~TH (REVISED JULY 8TH)

Love! All these sonnets about missing, missing—
What about love, *amor, amour—escucha,*
listen, *écoute,* we must have our "différance"
in order to love, to notice what is there—
How Joyce wrote of our lusting, raging bodies

If you don't feel it then pretend for god's sake
For the woman love is a matter of touch
Molly's yearning, her "Yes" our consolation
Remember the mind is full of old snowmen,
and arguments are games played on winter wounds

Underwent tempests, toyed with them, restated
them, saw beauty in the brave blue tragedy
and let it feed my exposed lopsided face
I hear the zeal of the sonnet, *escucha*

OCT. 9ᵀᴴ (FINISHED JULY 24ᵀᴴ)

Did you ever play the game of opposites?
"Mon Contraire est . . ." you uttered "coriaceous"
Never heard the fatty word so looked it up,
a leathery ferry—"My opposite is . . ."
What am I free from . . . the limits of my mind
a box of collections, a jar of jagged
contrary experience of other—Oh
Brother! Passersby look through the jalousie
& see children playing in front of a house
Really they fight in dry birdbaths and tears flow
The image which revealed nothing was grounded
in its avian inverse rising that is
the challenge of history: all remembered
a different game fixed in nomenclature

OCT. 10TH [WHEN A SONNET HAD TOO MANY WORDS]

The warning
came after—
No fig leaf
for the naked
Lost,
the sound escaped,
unraveled
childhood—
Lost,
surrounded by
that sentence,
embarrassed by
the moans,
saw it all

OCT. 13TH AND YOU FEEL IT IN THE BODY

Wind decapitates anemones, you can
turn heavy under the coil of enemies,
a Midas touch these thoughts, contaminating—
the way they bend warp infiltrate the flower,
carry the unnecessary and add weight
to this speed—feel it deep inside the body
No room for poetry, what space could be made
for such transparency—you remember then
fragile petals in the sunshine ricochet—
me nowhere where are my whereabouts where are . . .
Huge move just asking to . . . the way fall colors,
purple petals, make way for the cold season—
father placed a cookie once in a lunch bag—
The body lets seeds pour from these memories

OCT. 14TH

Nothing left, nothing to hide, nothing to fear,
thick time has no memories just your absence—
Say something, you never say anything, say
something sweet—Existence empty when you're not
around (there, the impulse for a love poem)
How to stand now "in the middle of a thing"?
Without a blanket, one can get cold and whine,
complain like the rest—You were the very first
then had to go and who got caught in between,
behind the bottles, hooked, disappeared behind
vowels and mixed something something very strong—
Your absence upsets my present inner life
How can anything be contained? An absence
of the sun darkens skies and smells portentous—

OCT. 15TH

If to color with a different palette
is to pretend—If a tipsy turntable
plays "Leaving on a Jet Plane" as he speeds then—
If the rage is to break the breaks of the old
then—If the grass, if the cows, if the green bus—
If speed gained the children's cry the momentum
then—it would have happened differently, on
a different bed—his wife wouldn't have hit him,
he wouldn't have sped, the children's cries wouldn't
have been heard and the flying over cattle
guards and swearing—would stop— "Oh babe I hate to"
So let's pretend there's a momentary breeze
Let the children sing, wave to the cows, and play
as trees converge on a country road—let them

OCT. 20TH

Move forward, don't doubt or deny poetry,   "   "
don't hold on to soft hands, the child holds on to   having to
the woman—Strike! A witness between indoor   outdoor
and nouns hidden behind broken thought patterns
This morning's bright cold moment, Here, Still, the light,
the loop sets the tone for reversals in time,
broadcast loops, but she knows better than to trust
what the news might say this morning about breeze—
washcloth soaked in warm water over the face
Strike! Predictions heat the noise needles, the whole
which holds to the promise of not I nor know   I
"Future" makes genuflecting impossible   Still here
"Weather" not quite right this morning—poetry   Even if
troubling when you try to predict the pattern   not the same

OCT. 21ST (VERSION 1)

for Danny

The theater's "dark," the actors/technicians wait
The play: A passenger on a subway—Scene:
An altercation that comes into focus
An arrival then departure a distress
The eye is placed on the play's "the thing" a ghost
where there are "no small parts only" a score played,
a set constructed to look like the "real thing"
where lines are measured blocked & rehearsed—actors
anticipate, long for *their* "Moment," they wait
memorize lines, their different perspectives
The leads are all men that's how it was written
Here on "the subway" the women are silent
Having written it he grabs hold of the lines,
having written it playwright forms the measure

OCT. 21ST (VERSION 2)

for Danny

An arrival, a departure, then distress
The passenger on the subway is a ghost,
gives the directions to this drama, the way
of heartache, the fiction of the large the small
the lie only we are lied to so often
The theater's dark, actors wait and technicians
measure lights to uncover blows that will come
"the thing is camouflaged so as to impress"
A set constructed to look as if "actual"
Having written them, the family hold lines,
mine and yours, here where the actors are silent
longing for *their* "Moment" anticipating
new parts new lines a different perspective
here where altercations comes into focus

OCT. 22ND

Write about black & white concave vertigo
in a crevice where naïveté met darkness,
met a director's vision of violence
of a different variety when used to
homemade via the hand no matter the day,
"copybook" kind everywhere not brave erased
ready to be thrown again by any word
or image "get out" which gripped but I sat there
fascinated behind whiteness foreignness
the resistance to a new stance copied out
as if frozen there in the samurai film
watched late at night in the quiet apartment
The scream reverberating in the silence
Mifune just committed hara-kiri

OCT. 24TH

What is unreal is how the rest of the day
disappeared into a silent waterfall
I felt the cacophony and snatched a breath,
learned to see the edge of everything through this
that country roads implode and that cattle guards
intensify the green Volkswagen bus fear
flying children's screams couldn't calm the speeding
seeds crushed under wheels going even faster
the man and woman fighting in the front seats
the bus flying everything in my arm ached
it follows that cows in the background looked up
to still my father we screamed at my mother
"Stop!" and the crying "Stop!" the abrupt stopping
Green bus trembling the cows went back to eating

~~OCT. 27~~TH (REVISED JAN. 28TH)

Either way it would be new to sing of love
with a "troubadour spirit" for this singer
The mind instead scratches the surface a blank
stare then scrawls a way into congested space—
Perhaps it's time to go without land the ship
passed by the statue and not at liberty
to say—blinded—in shock—the first view of it,
the teeming city—when moving is the main
attraction, and reaction to your suitcase—
the question repeated at the landing was
"When do we go back?" A new place to dock in
or to vacate before getting there—dislodged—
"When do we go back?" became *the* question
Sirens and height, on the rebound to nowhere

OCT. 29TH

It's madness this falling in love with sadness,
that faint sound a song that keeps resurfacing
between thoughts that Icarus carried too far
seen from the river's edge painting by Bruegel
She's able to swim with help from a large dog
(over and beyond tale of the falling youth)
I envy the comfort that she takes from him
(falling brusquely into a dream) bathed in a
sunlit world where "the whole pageantry" deepest
when at my desk voluntarily holding
"it" the absent, the falling, the dangerous
just balances at the edge of the tale, of
dangerous dropping places where "knights" "ladies"
plummet and cannot recover from madness—

~~OCT. 30~~TH (REVISED MARCH 20TH)

The images shift allegiance depending
on fraught contours of memory uncanny
defined by degrees of sensitivity—
bebop in the stillness, language grips borders
ill at ease in the stillness still children sleep
backstage, troubling scene of man shaking a cat
until it died (can't be erased once it's heard)—
in the background, turbulence is part turmoil
No cure for tiny world trembling all over
An autumn leaf falls tense shrieks in the hallway
mixed with laughter, sex, saxophone, flute playing,
then the lingering at a long wood table
Memory restless impatient with these scenes
especially the ones with faint foundation

OCT. 31ˢᵀ (VERSION 1)

Remove color, the walls of uncertainty—
palpable picture of an open valise
clearly facing forms of alienation
Obvious breakdown of the background vista
painted by one's own hand—I can remember
I wore heavy shoes, a wool coat and silence
in a narrow bed, no air, endless jerking
She was naked the young man on top eager
Girl an image in a movie pretending
while trying to fit the experience in,
to make sense of, grasp the pattern of pigeons
It's so discomforting the lack of color
black & white labels don't help the hot red cheeks
grab a handful of lies to make sense of it

OCT. 31ST (VERSION 2)

Preoccupation with portions, getting them
There were certain feelings but not exact words,
clearly not clear but desire embodied
a certain risk the breakdown of the background
painted by the right hand—I can remember
I wore heavy shoes, a wool coat and silence
in a narrow bed, no air, endless jerking
Being naked, a "nude," man on top eager
Girl in a movie pretending excitement
as she tried to fit the experience in
to make sense of, grasp the pattern of the fall
So discomforting knowing there was no love
Labels won't help the heart or books about it,
grabbing handfuls of lies to make sense of it

NOV. 4TH

When you forget to count syllables that's when
it's easy to retreat, no matter the day,
no matter the leaf blowers, the hammering,
last night's hurt—maintain the self under control—
How the mind goes, tries to squeeze everything in,
all the bad habits and wanting to confess—
No fire escape, a brick wall, tit for tat
Can't contain all that in a safe enclosure,
though could leave the terrible condemnations
behind the line, pull the weeds out of the bed
to see things for their silent transparency—
in the "Fairer House" Gauguin's "white horse" enters
In that full house liberty becomes pressing—
loan yourself to the task/trial of composure

NOV. 5TH ELECTION SONNET

A day of sounds, first nothing, then radiance—
the clamoring of horns, pots & pans, and cries
Winning is intense after the wait—these days
inching their way to vote—the jubilation
after resistance where grace takes an instant
Nothing less for the woman and her walker
exuberant, in line, electing the change—
a bird builds its nest from its saliva drop
by drop in dark caves—the delight of this day
will heal the tingling body, fill it with new
syllables, as we let go of old stiffness
The door for some will be weighty, but mostly
euphoria will crowd round new continents—
waited in line as for fancy bird's nest soup

NOV. 10TH

Shaken by the ventilation the season
in which direction is autumn now spinning
Watch how you season that meat it may bite you
or birth another change—reading in the dark
arc of childhood hallway connecting the child
to a warm hand and a riddle that reveals
we know nothing about love or know how to
—listen the line is traced, fettered by the form
the page where syllables tether the language
Can you gauge whether there will be enough to
go around, notice how to place/lace the words—
Parched, threatened by a dry wilderness woke up
The demands of memory a tendency
to mimic and invent a story early

~~NOV. 19~~TH (REVISED MARCH 26TH)

Not just about placement   but also the wait

Morning in winter, at the desk, brisk cold wind

"Unbearable," a word like that is heavy

Not to insist on what another can't give,

caves where echoes knot, chambers for everything,

everything, the exiled and past/present time

Besides the phrase shapes, undertakes a new day

The untidy disorganized mess of it

Not about saying something   but an instance

Having to wait, wait, and fill the space with it

Memory then of those phrases   now a cave

Their echoes knot, a chamber for everything,

every thing the exiled and the present time

The untidy disorganized mess of it

NOV. 24TH (FINISHED AUG. 3RD)

"Fool," said the heart, "start paying attention to
something"— affliction keeps me at a standstill,
the range of reality at an impasse,
an avocation flattened into gridlock
in my mind—under the quince tree, apple, pear,
tenderness passes by like mist in one's head

What of them in the streets, underneath a tree,
hands outstretched—what we give is inadequate—
"inadequate thinking" as Oppen would say
And the "shoppers"? . . . me not being able to
write it, clearly that's the barest minimum
Behind windows so as not to be disturbed
Is that how we separate ourselves, behind
the "Do Not Disturb" of our fragmentations?

NOV. 27TH

The holiday table is set, but outside . . .
I'm a marine they send you to the desert
they give you a wheelchair America can
you spare a little change for some'n to eat?
At least you got a home to go to you know
how quickly you could lose it right now you could
go home and it could be burned down to the ground
so easy you'd have lost it all lose your job
happens all the time can't even look at me
you can't even spare a little something for
someone who's homeless at least you got a home
Fuck trying to tell a grown man how to speak
Fuck I fought for this country and shit I'll speak
they gave me a wheelchair don't try and shush me

~~DEC. 4TH~~ (REVISED N.D.)

Screams in the building permeated with her
screams, no filtration system to mitigate
listening to the woman with Alzheimer's
Her "forever after" a bedtime lullaby
one camouflages by constant distraction—
not ready to listen to one's own nothing

The time wasted going shopping, not writing,
fruits and vegetables and the right amount
of sea salt to brine the words and sentences
Without a doubt matters of   saturation
My nucleus permeable   drained, hard, drips
Without a doubt a matter of   wayfaring
Words build a slick veneer around the thickness,
they disturb the strata and say what they mean

~~DEC. 10TH~~ AFTER THOMAS WYATT (REVISED FEB. 1ST)

Of being left behind being left alone,
of being shown up for less than what I was—
I wanted to win at all costs, clung tightly
to desire but dread/doubt conquered daring
Collision between what's wanted and dreaded
I was knocked out in the first round, fearful of
—will you still love me—went into the fable
to heal dissolution—   unbelievable
"dread and desire the reason doth confound"
Trepidation sets up sequences of of
(twenty-four hours later I'll think of what
to say) between bouts of misunderstanding
"I didn't mean that"   the unsayable given
The boomerang makes its way back as always

~~DEC. 11ᵀᴴ~~ (REVISED N.D.)

The first lesson is about the wind journey,
being quieted, learning to overcome—
a way out of phlegmatic calculations:
a + b = zero   or these fictions
we're asked to trust, just to be "agreeable"
In the silence, transform the somber shade &
succumb to traveling weather-exposed, no rest
now for the "cloud-moving wind" in the artist
Cold rain & modifications in white skies
In the city's signs, attractions show a lack
of concern for logic when it comes to what
truly matters—lack of concern for stymied
humans stuck in the static of recurrence—
On screens the day showered in calculations

DEC. 22ND

WINTER SOLSTICE

Morning movements saturated with sharp light
Lift an arm leg another turn one or two
parts of my body remain warm still, static
at this time of year turns are elliptical
When it's reached by subway a neighborhood seems
seasoned with shoppers, shaped by designers of
chocolate and bags, and lineups of iPods
Lights glitter this time of year, dark days ahead
in this Northern Hemisphere that's what happens,
as with making love, which happens late at night
Life my lease, read that Keats died in Italy
that day in February "writ in water"
and we keep on swimming, his words penetrate
the hours of darkness, the wonder of it

JAN. 18TH THE INAUGURATION

after the celebration patience with cold
snow in New York the economy is in
your face friend lost your job & another young
man in the subway HIV and thrown out
thrown into the market where another works
at two, uptown and midtown, minimum wage
is seven dollars and fifteen cents I see
at the cleaners I read that the death toll rose
to a thousand in the Holy Land the air
is heavy with it and I've made some tea nine
thirty a.m. and it's stopped snowing I can't
write a Frank O'Hara poem so I won't
try for "insouciance" though snow lands & a plane
lands softly in the middle of the Hudson

FEB. 9TH FOR SPENSER (VERSION 1)

Speak of illiteracy it's important!
I wish I could find clarity but the mind
is caught by too much emotion to think straight
When did the reading stop, when did the shame take
over so that nothing could be admitted
After mother fainted? When the dog was thrown?
The reading stopped, and the grief "unto you grew"
Emotional cracks in the big picture thrived
The wretchedness was real, etched and lingering,
warm shame warm like a friend a brother these bonds
that hold you captive, this imprisoning shroud
It doesn't hurt those who were too busy, too
full, too strained, to notice the burdensome needs
We don't read the same future, there, lots of snow

~~FEB. 11~~TH FOR SPENSER (VERSION 2, REVISED N.D.)

I wish I could find clarity but the mind
Blinded by burdensome needs a gust of wind
We don't read the same future, there, lots of snow
We don't read the same past, nothing admitted
Fainted into deep green when dishes were thrown
The reading stopped, the maelstrom "unto you grew"
When did the reading stop? On a sleepless night?
Emotional cracks in the big picture thrived
Accidents warm like a friend a brother bond
Enough palings to hold time captive, enough
Speak of illiteracy it's important!
The wretchedness was real, and behold lingered
Snow stirs up memories again of the past
I'm caught by too much emotion to think straight

MARCH 10TH (FINISHED AUG. 7TH, A YEAR LATER)

SONNET BEGINNING WITH LINE BY FANNY HOWE

Only that which exists can be spoken of
The buildings in New Jersey hidden by fog
Passersby on Broadway and 123rd
The air same here as at the seminary
Scribblings on a calendar reminder of
Dull sounds of a jackhammer in the morning
The character in the novel collapses
In the essay the poet writes of Auden
The man's body on the bus was much too close
Daffodils and squill, scaffolding and derricks
A bacteria present in the stomach
Atys in Lully's opera takes his own life
She was neater, better dressed, better preserved
Whatever is put down on paper later

~~OCT. 23~~RD MARCH 23RD

Designed to function during winter, building
the perceptual in letters, conversation
a practice that documented transactions—
something breaking open "to do something new"
to emerge from an aggregation of tropes
Made a mess of living, weren't we here and
not there, not in spatially blank narratives

In that outstretched hand the endangered one speaks
Ghosts emerge from the swinging doors of commerce
—in a long line "I" finally noticed "we"
lost, forgot everything, and alternatives
to magic will travel sitting on a chair
this day of seasons and illuminations
I head now to live in the explosive range

~~SEPT. 16TH~~ APRIL 7TH
FOR EDMUND SPENSER (VERSION 3)

"The living fire" begins with kindling, requires
rubbing sticks back and forth to grab attention
Words when they're specific start to signify
on paper our thoughts propel very quickly

The way we depend in the end on tension
when we look for despair rather than substance
We regard the world with such "base affections"
The writing will find us born where we question

The poet's habit to frame thoughts within form
How long do we have do we have do we have
to leave these dark storms that lead to estrangement

pushing lines of light to faraway borders
Language is beauty is passion is fire
I must fashion my self teach me that strangeness

~~SEPT. 16TH~~ APRIL 7TH
FOR EDMUND SPENSER (VERSION 3)

APRIL ~~10~~ᵀᴴ (REVISED N.D.)

SONNET BEGINNING WITH LINE BY HOPKINS

"I wake and feel the fell of dark, not day" these
stark times spent in solitary listening
You sharpest whirlwind witness of "my mean life"
(was meant to make something of it, not squash it)

Talk of the hours the years and countless cries
the ritual (damn) the desolate forsaken
You know where wide wings sequester, assemble
loaded labor thrives on clarification

"The lost are like this" forever criss-crossing
(was meant to take the wreckage and intone it)
Furious with this agitation, no justice

where oppressed the unsayable (crap) snaps days
of goodness (was meant to, meant to, meant to jump)
Crookedness has a dull way of sipping tea

APRIL 13TH AFTER SOPHOCLES

How could I fail to see the father/brother
blind—forgets, tries to remember the riddle,
to remember *the ancient guilt,* so hard to—
I'll bring it all to light myself—hunted, tracked
I curse myself—Who remembers what happened?
There was a riddle   a family riddle
Remember all that force—*the blind old man can*
Temper, fury, the monarch then *brought all down*
in his strong arms   *to solve the mystery of*
to *see the truth at last* before shrinking, thin
skin hangs   to *see my origins face to face*
(The pains we inflict upon ourselves hurt most)
Let my destiny come   so much left behind
I hear weeping   marked in the ground left behind

AUG. 4ᵀᴴ APRIL 15ᵀᴴ

Flag in the wind and a leafless tree gives pause
to the mind that can never quite know enough
to see how shades of gray sky have now shifted
The mind too occupied with past and future
retreats into itself, its fluctuations
Without body how will words slip from the pen?
So much uncertainty and then the poem . . .
What do we hunt today? What song do we trail?
Kept running into poems, one by Oppen,
one by Wyatt, shifts of form bedding down with
"this in which," the discovery of the "here,"
of the animal, small and startled, eyes wide
at attention my body, your deer body,
both are like the day, slipping away, passing

APRIL 16ᵀᴴ STILL LIFE

Flowers in a jar, stem leaves petals purple

A place to return to where the room is red

A teapot on the table, red tablecloth,

apples in a basket placed near a mirror

Returning to the scene becomes primal scene

Approached the window for a breath of fresh air

away from the bowl of orange-red apples

A man, a woman and a child in-between

wanted to please both—sea sounds in that warm sun

shaped by the line, placed, the stillness of what is

in the scene the damage was brought to a head

in the mirror your self-portrait your figure

your ordinary every day face stares back

The subject lies in the marks of a paintbrush

~~JULY 17~~TH APRIL 23RD

"Clarity!" elusive as ever in these
sonnets the unmanageableness of them,
keeping tracks well covered just in case order
stops being able to tell us anything
So much pressure in the form so I worry
Rain seeps in the dream the door is half-open
down "dark alleys" of thought I quietly hide
What kind of life and in relation to what
The computer, the screen, the impervious
Not everyone I know can handle the scorched
Perhaps it will get printed someday that is
just when I'm about to collapse I'll see it
and have to start all over begin again
inside mortality my only dwelling

Acknowledgments

Some of the sonnets are "in conversation," directly or indirectly, with the following: John Berryman, Dante Alighieri, Ted Berrigan, Dylan Thomas, William Wordsworth, William Butler Yeats, Anne Winters, Sir Thomas Wyatt, W. H. Auden, Bernard Noël, Gerald Manley Hopkins, Thomas Hardy, Stéphane Mallarmé, John Milton, William Shakespeare, Sir Philip Sidney, Laynie Browne, John Donne, Samuel Taylor Coleridge, Wallace Stevens, Matsuo Bashō, Inger Christensen, Arthur Rimbaud, Jacques Roubaud, William Carlos Williams, George Oppen, Bernadette Mayer, Mark Jarman, Gwendolyn Brooks, Alice Oswald, George Herbert, Michael Palmer, Edmund Spenser, Percy Bysshe Shelley, Robert Duncan, Charles Baudelaire, and my father.

Many thanks and appreciation to the editors of the following journals where versions of some of these poems first appeared: *The Nation, Drunken Boat, Try, Zoland Poetry #5, Zen Monster, Catch-Up,* and *Upstart; A Journal of English Renaissance Studies.*

I am grateful to Carol Snow, Gabrielle Civil, and Russell Switzer for their insights and suggestions, along with Camille Guthrie and Joshua Beckman for their encouragement. I also wish to thank the Sisters at The Abbey of Regina Laudis for their indefatigable inspiration and hospitality. Finally I want to extend my gratitude to Susan Stewart for choosing *Scaffolding* for the Princeton Series of Contemporary Poets, and to express my sincere thanks to everyone at Princeton University Press for making this book possible.

·